Pagan Portals
Hedge Witchcraft

Pagan Portals
Hedge Witchcraft

Harmonia Saille

Winchester, UK
Washington, USA

First published by Moon Books, 2012
Moon Books is an imprint of John Hunt Publishing Ltd., Laurel House, Station Approach,
Alresford, Hants, SO24 9JH, UK
office1@jhpbooks.net
www.johnhuntpublishing.com
www.moon-books.net

For distributor details and how to order please visit the 'Ordering' section on our website.

Text copyright: Harmonia Saille 2011

ISBN: 978 1 78099 333 1

The rights of Harmonia Saille as author have been asserted in accordance with the Copyright,
Designs and Patents Act 1988.

A CIP catalogue record for this book is available from the British Library.

Design and cover photograph: Stuart Davies

Printed and bound by CPI Group (UK) Ltd, Croydon, CR0 4YY

We operate a distinctive and ethical publishing philosophy in all
areas of our business, from our global network of authors to
production and worldwide distribution.

CONTENTS

Dedication

For my friend Edmund (Cusick) 1962–2007

Introduction

The Hedge Witch

Hedge witchery in general is experiential and a slow and natural progression of interests and events often experienced from childhood and persisting all through your life. As Aristotle said, 'For the things we have to learn before we can do them, we learn by doing them.'

Learning by experiencing is about trusting your instincts and connecting with your inner spirit.

There is no dogma attached to hedge witchcraft. There are no tenets to follow. And if you asked a hundred hedge witches what their practice is, you will get a variety of different answers. The path of a hedge witch is very much an individual one, and it is a solitary practice. In this way, this book is based on my own experiences as a hedge witch living in Ireland and following a Celtic path.

In general, hedge witches base their practices on those of the cunning people and wise folk of old. They often gain ideas from historical texts on how cunning people would practice and garner spells and brews from them. However, these are adapted, as I personally do not put dead cats in my walls or pee in a bottle.

However, no matter how hard we wish it or how hard we try, we cannot be like the witch, cunning, or wise person of old. Modern witchcraft and paganism are exactly that 'modern'. Hedge witchcraft too is a modern and individual practice. My ancestors did not pass down their practice in a secret book of shadows nor did my granny teach me it. Just as much as the old ways and equipment belonged to the witch of old, modern ways and equipment belong to our time and so do we. We cannot live in the past and why would we want to, life is easier for us than it was for those living in previous centuries. However, we keep the spirit of the old witch alive in the modern craft.

Confucius was reported to have said, 'Tell me, and I will forget. Show me, and I may remember. Involve me, and I will understand.' This book will show you something of a Celtic hedge witch's path whether that is a walk out in nature or a hedgeriding experience. *Hedge Witchcraft* is a book where you will go about *experiencing* what it is to be a hedge witch. Hedge witch*craft* is exactly that, a *craft*. A modern apprenticeship is generally four-fifths practical work and one-fifth theory. And like an apprenticeship, Hedge Craft is a hands-on experience with eighty percent practice and twenty percent reading.

With a love of nature, a hedge witch is truly a pagan like any other, but what makes us a hedge witch are the more simple ways we follow that have more meaning than any complicated rituals.

I wrote this book at the request of readers of my earlier books, as through these are scattered various aspects of hedge witchcraft. Here I pull together all the information into one book, adding to and extending the knowledge.

Pagan Portals — Hedge Witchcraft will guide you if you wish to read more about hedge witchcraft as a pathway, or are already following such a path and wish to progress. It only has a little about hedge riding as this book has too small a scope to include it. Please read my accompanying book in the Pagan Portal series, *Hedge Riding*.

What do Hedge Witches Do?

As a hedge witch, your personal interests may include nature, herbs, folk magic, divination, healing and most particularly, hedge riding. Similar to most pagans, you will carefully watch the seasons change and celebrate them with festivities, from the first signs of rebirth in the spring to the ripeness of summer, to the collecting in of the sustainable harvest, and the resting period of the dark winter months. You will most likely follow the waxing and waning of the moon and tides and do not wish for the end of one season and reject the start of another often with negativity (as with winter), but accept each one and attempt to flow with them.

As an animist and pantheist, you may see divinity in all things without and within with a guardian spirit inhabiting each lake, stream, hill and mountain, plant and tree.

As a solitary witch, you do not have to be lonely and so there is no need to confine yourself to the house and secretly go about your witchy business. You can network regularly with other witches and pagans and meet up with them when you can. You can perhaps attend moots, rituals and gatherings and share your experiences with others. Maybe swap recipes for herbs and wildflowers, swap seeds and superfluous plant cutting, and learn new methods and new ways of cooking more healthily. The benefits though of hedge witchery is being able to 'do your own thing', such as growing herbs and vegetables, or walking out in nature to talk to nature spirits, or to watch the wildflowers appear and collect items for the occasional folk spell.

As a hedge witch, it is better to go out and *experience*

nature than sit in, think and read constantly. A 'sense of place' is therefore paramount to spirituality. There is nothing better than to detach yourself from the busy, noisy and crowded towns, and lose yourself in the tranquility and the almost surreal, non-materialism of the landscape. You will find a natural sacred space within the forest, on the hill or close to the lake. While lost in your landscape, and quoting a dear friend the late academic and poet Dr Edmund Cusick, you may well experience the same feeling:

> ...I still feel essentially lifted up in spirit when I pull up at the head of the Glen, get out and breathe in. It is mountain country, as surely as the Cairngorms is — the absolute sense that this is no longer human territory, but the territory of the wilderness, that the animals, the trees, are the natural inhabitants and that we do not primarily belong there.
>
> (Between Field and Stars, Headland 2008)

When we are in the countryside we too, often, feel the wild otherness of the spirit there, and that we are privileged to be there — but then this is the natural and magical territory of the hedge witch, so we stay.

The Lake

Thistles and nettles scratch at my legs
impeding my progress, as I find my hillside settle.
Ahead the sun strikes stone, through the ash tree,
a dazzling diamond, reflecting in the smoothness of the lake.
Echoing in the distance is the flap of a swan's wings
as it flails in reeds, and the blatant buzz of the fly
as it catches in my tangled hair.
Barbed whitethorn stands queenly among weeds,

where swallows swoop, while blue damsel hovers
around solitary rose, lost in the gamut of greenness.
Glass hills sit neatly on the horizon like a child's drawing,
distant, unreal, unreachable.

I see the river as it leaves the lake,
winding to the land of possibilities,
open to all who seek.
I see the wind now as it blows like waves of horizontal
rain pouring across forbidden landscape.
Sentinel whitethorn scatters her offspring below,
watching. I hear the wind whisper, trees talking,
birds singing as the swan princess glides
over the rippling slate, where her human lover awaits.
Silky sylphs veiled in feathered cloud
float in and out of the blue. Fabled fairy sails
around my feet, beckoning as the wind blows
her to the tree of life and her dazzling diamond.
Solitary wild rose her pretty head bowed, reaching
seeking.

I reach out and touch the hills.

Connecting with Nature

Connecting with nature is becoming a part of it. It is the need
to see yourself as a small part of the whole of nature and it
will make all the difference to the way you not just view but
see things. See the landscape as Edmund saw it, and observe
the absolute sense that it is no longer human territory. Lose
yourself in the landscape. See nature as belonging to no one,
owned by none, not by the farmer or the landowner, the inhab-
itant, or the state or country. Nature exists above and beyond
the land. Land may be territory but nature is spirit, nature is
free, uncontrollable, mutable, wild, serene, terrifying,

beautiful, devastating, magnificent, joyful, destructive, and life-giving. Loving nature is accepting the wild along with the serene, the destructive along with the life giving aspects of it.

When people say they pit themselves against nature, perhaps mountain climbing or white water rafting, they cannot actually control or conquer nature, only survive it. However, in doing so they become a part of nature and they go with it — adapt to it, rather than go against it. They are companions to nature. When we walk in the fields or paddle in the stream we can also be a companion — adapt ourselves to our surroundings, and become a part of and go with nature, without putting ourselves at risk I might add.

When out in nature employ all your senses. Look around you and *see*. By *see*, I mean really look to see what is there. You will be surprised at what you miss when you walk and your mind wanders to everyday matters. Keep your concentration, look at everything, and acknowledge what you see. Look at the texture of the bark or leaves, the different shades of green, the breeze kissing the blades of grass, the trout meandering in the stream, and the squirrel scurrying up the tree trunk. Listen to the tinkling of the water as it musically winds its way down the rocks, or the birds singing, trees whispering or the ocean sighing.

When you touch something, you directly connect with it. Feel the rough bark of the tree, or the velvet of the rose petal. Feel the breath of wind in your hair, or the coldness of the water as you dangle your feet in the stream, or the softness of the grass as you run barefoot in the meadow.

Hum, sing or whistle as you join the sounds of nature.

Sense the spirit of place, the spirit in the mountain, the spirit in the stream, the spirit in the tree or rock.

Over the years, you may have never connected with nature owing to modern demands on your time and person. As a result, you may well have drawn a line between nature and yourself. Therefore, when you travel through the countryside, to the park, or even if you step into your garden, you see it all as something separate, like a theme park you visit and then leave. Try to remove that line that lies between you and the hills, the lakes, rivers and oceans, the trees, the flora and fauna, the rose and the song thrush or at least blur it. Step into the inside instead of on the outside looking in. The exercise below is designed to help you do just that.

Exercise
Shapeshift into nature by becoming what you see. See the tree and become it by slipping into it so that your legs and feet become the roots, your body the trunk and your head the branches. Feel and hear what is going on inside you, the sap rising, the insects burrowing, the wind swaying your branches and rustling your leaves.

Become part of the swan on the lake or river, preen your feathers and swim majestically with the other swans. After a while, slip into the water as a droplet and become part of it, liquidize yourself. After a short time, you are no longer a droplet but a part of a much larger whole, the lake that leads into the river, which leads in to the ocean, which is a part of the earth, in turn a part of the universe.

More on a Sense of Place
A personal 'sense of place' is one in which we feel we belong and with which our identity is irrevocably tied. We have a deep attachment and connection to this place. Activities such as playing there as a child, walking or working there as an adult, unite with meaning that we gain from this place. The 'place' might be a country, a particular area or landscape, or even a town or village. When we experience a sense of place, we have a sense of coming home and belonging and of being

content and we are at our most happy when we are there.

Your sense of place may well be within particular landscapes of rivers, lakes, the sea, hills, mountains, valleys, fields and forest. It may well have a connection with your ancestors. Yet it does not have to be in the countryside, but in a park, gardens, or even in the city.

For example, many people of Irish descent grew up with a sense of their Irishness along with tales of the 'old country'. Many of them will retain their Irish family name. These sons and daughters of Ireland often feel they belong in Ireland rather than their own or as well as their own country. Their ancestors would not have had to leave Ireland if it was not for the struggles during the famine years or during times of extreme hardship. Many Irish people understand this, accept and welcome these stray sons and daughters and fully understand their connectedness to this country and may nod and say, 'Of course you do. What else?' These Irish people are often very much connected and attached to their land and so expect others to be so. They have the same 'sense of place' as their visitors. And if we visit the 'old country' we immediately feel we are 'coming home'.

We use all our senses when connecting with our 'place'. You see the landscape, smell the grass, trees and flora, listen to the running water and the wind rustling through the trees, pick fruit or drink the spring water. You touch the grass or dangle your feet in the stream and feel the rain on your face and during all this your sixth sense or intuition is heightened.

We have a physical experience with our 'place' but also a spiritual one, for a sense of place is coalesced with spirituality.

Exercise

Take a pen and paper and write on it the places that resonate with you. It may only be one place but could be several. What draws you to this place or these places? If there is more than one place, is there a link between them? If it is only one place, what happened there that made it so significant? If you cannot reach this place easily, stop writing, close your eyes, and try to connect with it. Bring in the memories that accompany it. Is part of you still there? Make a vow to visit the place as soon as you can, if you cannot do this, then go to it within a visualization exercise. Visiting it can bring you happiness, contentment and peace.

Spirit of Place

Part of the feeling of a 'sense of place' is an awareness of the 'spirit of place'. A pagan friend and ex-pat American said that when she arrived in Ireland she no longer felt connected to her previously chosen gods and goddesses, but instead had a growing need to connect with the Celtic gods and goddesses of Ireland and also of the area.

In Ireland, there is a strong sense of spirit in the landscape, the wells, portals, stone circle, raths, lakes, rivers, sea, forest and many other places, and it is easy to understand the need to connect with them. There are many aspects of folklore and mythology connected with certain areas such as counties, mountains, rivers or lakes and many books have been written about them. Folk songs and poems immortalize places and people, which all help to promote a potent sense of the spirit of place. Alternatively (or perhaps additionally), it may well be our connection to our own ancestral spirits that evoke the spirit of place.

Needless to say, this is not unique to Ireland. There are many places and other countries such as mainland Europe, the UK, US, Africa and Australia, which have a powerful spirit of place.

'Spirit of place' and a 'sense of place' are related in that it is difficult to experience one without the other. They go hand in hand — and are an essential part of pagan spirituality.

When you experience your sense of place and view the valley, forest, river and hills around your home be aware of your relationship with creation and that you are part of that creation, a single continuity — and therefore have your place in the universe. All is sacred and one. There is no fundamental difference between the earth under your feet and the sacred place or site you visit — your 'place' is essentially every bit as important. You will feel the presence of the divine in the landscape of your 'place' and find it so much easier to connect out of doors than in.

Exercise
When visiting your 'place' either in actuality or in a visualization exercise, stop for a moment and see if any particular deity or nature spirit calls to you. Perhaps the ancestors are calling to you. Who is connected with this place? When you go to your place, make it a point to find out. Call to the mountains, the river, the meadows, call to the ancestors, the nature spirits and the gods and goddesses that belong there.

There is spirit in all things, so at your place touch the rocks, trees, grass and plants (this could be in a garden or park), put your hands in the soil, touch and connect with the earth.

Sense of the Divine
When you are sentient to nature, you view it more *divinely* every time you go out. You become more aware that we are indeed one with nature (clichéd as it may seem). You view yourself as a speck in nature as is the tree or the leaf.

While writing this part of the book, the Cailleach oversees Munster — the leafless trees affording a clearer view of the Cailleach's landscape. It is good to appreciate more the Cailleach's time of year instead of wishing for the warmth of spring. In addition, instead of looking back to wasted years, it is good to enjoy the *now* years.

As well as the Cailleach in the winter, I equate the other seasons with the goddesses Brigid, Áine and Danu. You of course will have your own pantheon and particular god/s and goddess/es

The god aspect appears for me in nature and in the seasons. The god is the sun which gives life, he is the sky and the wind which carries the seed and deposits it on the land, he is the forest and the snow, is half of the fauna and the flora, the mountains and cliffs, and the four directions, north, south, east and west. The god is in and of nature.

You may find this concept difficult to grasp but for me it all comes together as one whole under the guise and wings of Mother Nature herself. Sorting out deity can take years but finally it comes together.

Whether man or woman it may take you years to understand your sense of the divine, the time when your deity will become clearer to you. Finding and understanding deity is not something to be rushed. In time, this will come to you. One day you will wake up and the understanding will come not as a revelation as if being struck by a flash of lightning, but as a gentle and gradual dawning as the sun creeps over the horizon and the twilight becomes day.

Hedge Riding

Many people call themselves hedge witches but the true hedge witch will practice the main feature of hedge witchcraft — hedge riding. Below I have explained only a little about it, and if you want to learn more about this, there is an accompanying book to this in the Pagan Portal series, called *Hedge Riding*.

The 'hedge' in 'hedge witch' has more than one meaning. Primarily the hedge is the boundary separating this world and the otherworld, the hedge witch crosses the hedge to explore the realms of the otherworld. The hedge is also both psychically and physically protective, keeping out unwanted visitors, spirit or human.

Hedge riding is shamanic in nature and is usually solitary as the hedge witch is solitary, but there is no reason why you cannot practice with others.

When hedge riding, the hedge rider's consciousness travels to another place, the otherworld, which is also the realm of the collective unconscious. There she or he encounters archetypal symbols and assimilates this knowledge to help guide her or him on their pathway.

Riding to the spirit realms is achieved by entering an altered state of consciousness, by such methods as drumming, drugs, fasting, dancing, or whatever personally suits you.

When you are truly hedge riding, although your body is in this world, it is your spirit consciousness that is in the otherworld.

The otherworld has three realms, which in themselves can have levels. I access the three worlds through a tree, which is the *Axis Mundi* and a connection between our own world and the otherworld.

Animal guides (often called the power animal or companion animal), play an important part in hedge riding. You do not choose your animal guides, but rather they have always been with you and they just appear to you having previously been invisible. So, although you might imagine that a wolf, bear, eagle or stag is your animal guide, it could well turn out to be a hare, turtle, or even an elephant.

Your animal companion can run, walk, swim, or fly beside you. The companion is company for you so you do not feel alone. It will give you strength, confidence and added protection.

You will also meet spirit guides when you hedge ride and

they come in all shapes and forms and are an added form of protection and guidance in the otherworld. More often presenting themselves in human form, they can appear in many guises, usually one that is comfortable for you.

The hedge witch rides to the otherworld to seek help from the spirits and elementals that reside there for healing, strength, spiritual enlightenment, protection, sometimes simply to look for messages or solutions to problems, for help in spell work and knowledge, but mostly to gain wisdom.

You should be an experienced hedge witch, be familiar with pathworking, or have followed some sort of shamanic course before you attempt to hedge ride. In *Hedge Riding*, you will find information on how to hedge ride and what you might experience in the otherworld and why hedge witches actually go there.

Ritual Tools

An athame, chalice, sword, cords — do they have a place in hedge witchcraft? When you go out into nature, you do not need any of these. All you need is you. For indoors, try to keep things simple. Altars or Craft tables may resemble the childhood nature table and contain items collected while out in nature, such as feathers, pebbles, shells, leaves, branches, sprigs of rowan or holly and many more such items. You may find a small cauldron or dish handy for burning incense. Wands can simply be small branches collected from nature, and left as they are: no adornments, no sanding, no varnishing. Of course, what is a witch without her besom?

In addition, you may want to keep a stock of charcoal for burning incense, a variety of candles, a smudge stick, a pair of scissors, a knife for cutting, ribbons and a number of other odds and ends such as a bell or shaman rattle.

In your spiritual space, you may keep jars of herbs, some

perhaps homegrown, some picked from out in nature and dried, or failing that bought, along with some resins and incenses, crystals and essentials oils. It is usual for a hedge witch to use divination and you may have a crystal ball, scrying mirror, sets of runes, tarot or dowsing rods.

You practice a Craft and therefore any items you use are part of that Craft. You do not need to go out and buy expensive and manufactured wands, chalices and other tools. As much as possible comes from nature, failing that a charity shop, or even items found around the home. This makes them much more personal and meaningful.

Familiars

In past times, witches' familiars were said to be messengers of the devil by Christian persecutors. In fact, anything that hung around the witch could be termed a familiar either wild or domesticated such as a toad, crow, cat or dog. Failing the presence of any actual animal then the witch was deemed to have an unearthly creature for a familiar such as an imp or demon. The witch was thought to transform herself into the familiar to go about doing her wicked deeds, often cursing or causing the deaths of animals and people.

Modern witches often find that an animal attaches itself to her, especially during magical practices. This will be a cat, dog, frog, rat or toad, but many witches (in fact pagans) have ravens and crows as constant visitors to their homes. A familiar could be any kind of creature, often wild, sometimes domesticated. These would include birds of any kind, small wild animals such as squirrels and insects such as bees.

The important thing is that you have a spiritual connection to this creature. Mentally the familiar can help in spell work by carrying messages into the otherworld. Alternatively, it will enhance spiritual connections during rituals.

Recognizing your familiar is fairly straightforward. The

animal will insist on sitting outside the window as you work, or will demand to be admitted into the room. You will have a close personal connection to this creature, more so than other family members. When you think of it, it will often appear at that moment. When you are upset or lonely, again it will often turn up to comfort you or give you a moment of lightness in the dark.

Begin slowly working with the familiar until you are sure that is what it is.

Sometimes, the familiar may die or disappear, and it might be some time before you make a connection with another. Making a connection is not something that can be rushed, nor can you force an animal to be your familiar. The animal needs to be willing. If it any time the animal no longer wishes to be your familiar, you will soon get to know, as it will stay away from your magical workings.

2

The Celtic Festivals

As a pagan, you may well follow the Celtic festivals, even if you follow another pantheon. As a hedge witch on a Celtic path, I do follow these festivals. Below is a little about each festival and ideas for celebrating.

Samhain

At Samhain, the pagan New Year, the apple strongly features and I will make dishes containing apple for the family and friends that I invite, as for me, this is a family occasion. When I was a child, we did not call this festival Hallowe'en but 'Duck Apple Night', as for our family it was mostly about the apple. We did make turnip lanterns though and were aware that faeries, ghosts and spirits abounded.

You can use parts of this celebration below to suit yourself as a solitary practitioner, or you can bring in family or friends to join in the festivities.

Here we begin the evening with a ritual in which everyone contributes and which features welcoming the Cailleach. The Cailleach transforms from Danu, the Autumn Queen into the Crone who brings with her the darkness and eventual death, just as Nature is now in her dark phase and everything rests and becomes dormant.

At Samhain, we think about those loved ones who have passed over and with the veil between the worlds at its thinnest, we feel them around us.

Often I have a theme for Samhain, and one year I lit candles for each of the young people I knew who passed away well before their time, these loved ones and friends ranged from babies to the age of thirty. Another year, I honored those who passed over prematurely in their middle years and another those loved ones who passed away in their later years. A few years ago, I invited some friends around and we chose a single person to remember. As a couple of the people had lost their beloved partners when they were still relatively young, it was indeed a sad time. Still, everyone experienced something profound and spiritual that night.

Choose a simple ritual to begin with, cast a circle if that is what you like to do, light some candles, all hold hands and say a few words, invite nature spirits, the god and goddess to join you. Remember your loved ones that have passed away, those dear to you, or perhaps honor your ancestors.

After this, you can settle down for some traditional activities. For my family and friends, we might each cut an apple in half and make five wishes on the star within. We may also indulge in the old tradition of duck apple also called bobbing for apples, in which we put apples in a bowl of water and catch them with our teeth. Additionally, we might hang apples from strings and try to catch them too with our teeth. This is an enjoyable festivity for adults as well as children. The roasting of chestnuts brings a certain nostalgia to the air. We finish by inviting everyone to leave a gift out for the faery folk who are close to our own world at this time.

As we approach winter and the wheel turns once more, we can look back on what we have accomplished throughout this year and can take time out to examine our lives and reflect on what we want to achieve the following year.

Nature takes a rest at this time of year and prepares to revitalize for the coming spring, we too as a part of nature can also take time out to rest, take stock of our lives, and rejuvenate our mind, body and spirit. The dormant months are the best time for recharging our batteries, making plans, perhaps even transforming ourselves. As winter freezes the external, we can go more deeply within ourselves to look for warmth.

Many people feel low during the winter or even depressed as it goes on, but just as it is true that the leaves on the trees die off, the tree itself lives and taking rest is secretly rejuvenating. If we see ourselves as much a part of nature as the tree, then we too can let some things go while planning how things can be so very different for us in the future. Looking forward to this can fill us with a glowing optimism. For some reason I see this optimism as the color yellow. And in spring nature does not let me down when suddenly there is yellow everywhere I look and the warmth of the sun touches my soul.

The Winter Solstice (Yule)

Yule is a family celebration, which includes the decorating of the home with holly and ivy. I love to go out and collect this in myself. We do not need a traditional Yule tree as we have plenty in our garden and back onto pine forest. My views have changed over the years and I would much rather see a tree growing to an immense height, than dying in a pot in my living room. There are of course the smaller live trees in pots, which you can later plant out if you have the space. To make our Yule tree we go out to find a number of fallen branches and spray them with silver and snow and place in a pot. We hang on this silver and glass baubles to some white faery lights. This is something that my mother did every year and it truly looks beautiful and attracts many comments.

On the morning of Yule, I wrap up warmly and will go out to my altar and welcome in the light of the waxing year. I remember that within a few short weeks the first snowdrops will appear followed by the first buds of spring.

Again, I connect with and honor the Cailleach, who grows even older, and soon will die and be reborn, as the earth will be reborn and new growth begins.

At Yule, I also connect with Gráinne a local goddess and faery queen and welcome the coming of the light. For it is good to have light to brighten the midwinter. I am lucky to have local goddesses to relate to so it is important to honor them albeit briefly at Yule.

January is generally a harsh month for many unless you live in the Southern Hemisphere. If you have not done so already, then take some time out now to take stock of your life. It is said that the mirror reflects the soul and only tells the truth. Winter is a good time to take time out to scry. We can do this with a black mirror, a black bowl filled with water, a crystal, or crystal ball (more about this in the divination chapter later in the book). Images may come to us symbolically or in actuality. And as we examine the meanings, we are also examining ourselves. As we search into the dark depths, we can carefully search for what should not be there but is rearing its ugly head. This will help with the clearing out process in readiness for spring.

When taking stock of ourselves we first need to remember who we are, the real us, only then can we examine our personal baggage and clear away the junk. Next, we can reorganize our thoughts, prioritize, and make decisions on what is really important in our lives. Once done, we will find it easier to connect. That is to connect with our inner self, with spirit, and with our personal practice. We will also find we connect more naturally with others.

Winter is not so bad after all. After the long rest and reflection, in the twinkling of an eye Mother Nature will dust herself off and come to life once more, vibrantly blossoming, glowing, vigorous and alive. We can do no better than to follow her excellent example.

Imbolg

At Imbolg, I connect with the goddess Brigid. Imbolg is the time of year when the first signs of spring appear and I say goodbye to the Cailleach as she gradually retreats with the winter. Representing the rebirth of the earth in spring, the Cailleach dies and is reborn as Brigid the maiden. At this time, I might make a Brigid's cross, but most certainly I will celebrate new beginnings. Also a celebration of hearth and home, I light an indoor fire and many candles.

A lovely walk is the order of the day to spot the buds forming on the trees such as the whitethorn. Often at this time of year, there is snow or frost on the ground. Yet at times, we suddenly get lovely February sunshine, which reminds us of the coming spring and adds a touch of optimism to our outlook. Soon flowers will push through the ground, such as snowdrops, swiftly followed by crocuses, daffodils, coltsfoot, lesser celandine and ground ivy.

Often there is snow on the ground to whiten our world or heavy frost to decorate the trees. Still, we know that spring is not far away.

At Imbolg, if you have not already done so then it is the last of the best times to de-clutter and spring-clean your home, your mind and your life — a time to clean out the old to make way for the new. After taking stock and making plans in the darker months, we can now begin to put them into action.

The home benefits from a spring clean to shake away the winter dust and grime. It is not only the home that needs de-cluttering but also the items in it, such as the computer and our wardrobes. Doing this in turn help us in de-cluttering our lives.

To de-clutter your mind, go for a walk, figure out what is worrying you the most in life and decide to either let it go as there is nothing you can do about the situation or determine to do something about it. If it is finances that are worrying you, decide to live more simply for a while, forget that you cannot have a holiday this year, but plan to holiday at home instead. Sort out what you can and cannot pay and arrange small payments, something is better than nothing. If a health problem is bothering you, why not go and get it sorted out.

In de-cluttering your life, sometimes change is in order, for nothing will magically change for us, we have to take those steps for ourselves even if they are only baby steps to start with. Try to gain the sense of optimism that spring brings us. Positive thoughts attract positive things.

Some myths tell us that Brigid (various spellings) is the daughter of the Celtic faery ruler or sun god the Dagda of the Tuatha Dé Danann. The Dagda, also according to certain myths, was born of *Bile* the oak tree together with the goddess *Danu* who watered it. Brigid is the patron of the fire, the forge, the hearth, craftsmanship (especially blacksmiths), poetry, childbirth and healing. Brigid is a fire goddess but is also linked with water. Imbolg, her day of celebration on the 1st/2nd of February, heralds the start of spring when fertility begins to return to the land. Brigid is the patron of poets and a goddess of inspiration. She also has connections with Excalibur and the Lady of the Lake, and is a shape-shifter and enchantress. Brigid is a midwife and healer and her healing waters are in the wells and streams, although she has connections with rivers and lakes too.

Each year I make a special altar for Brigid. This year I had a picture of the goddess an artist friend gave me and pictures of the hare (on cards given to me by friends). In addition, I have tea lights in spring-decorated candleholders (grass, ladybirds and rabbits), a piece of birch bark, yellow and white candles, snowdrops (picked) and daffodils (bought) and one or two other small items from nature.

My Imbolg altar is a simple one with just an incense

burner, candlesnuffer and my birch wand as tools. It is an altar of new beginnings reflecting the first sign of growth out in nature. On my walk, I did indeed find those signs in buds on the trees.

In a simple ritual, I ask Brigid for protection for my family and friends. I prepare the room by cleaning it and take a cleansing bath or shower with salt and cleansing herbs.

I prepare my altar so that it is facing east and spiritually cleanse the area with my besom and sprinkle the floor with lavender or sage.

I think of the purpose of the ritual and light the candles. After lighting my incense, I invite the protective nature spirits to join me. I then politely invite Brigid to attend my ritual by saying my own prayer of invitation as follows:

O Brigid of the sacred spring
Bless me, keep me under thy wing
Let your sacred mantle cloak me
Protect and guard me from dark entity

O Brigid the eternal fire
With words of wisdom please inspire
With knowledge and vision please bestow
So that with your blessing I may grow

O Brigid of the secret smile
Please come to me and bide awhile
With me, in me, your perpetual light
Will fill me, guide me, in this rite.

I then sit and think about what those new beginnings will be. This could be a house move, a new book or project, a new way of doing things, or perhaps a new way of conducting myself in my daily life. If a loved one needs help, I also ask for it. I continue the celebration with food and drink.

To end, I thank the spirits for attending and guarding me. I finish by sweeping up the lavender or sage. I leave the candles burning (always of course keeping a watch on them). If the moon is new or waxing to full, I might burn the candles down over three days.

The Spring Equinox

At the Spring Equinox, I honor the coming fertility of the land and Brigid remains my goddess of the season as the maiden coming into full bloom. Mother Nature brings us an evolution of beauty, fertility is abounding and lambing season has begun. Insects begin to appear again, and on sunny days we begin to hear the buzzing of the bumblebee, while the birds appear to sing all the louder. We know that at this time of year there is still a risk of snow, but we soon see the blades of grass peeping up through the whiteness, and know that it will be short lived and next week we could be out without our coats and jackets.

In March, I bring out my pottery eggs and chicks and bunnies to place around the house to signify fertility and rebirth. Spring is here now with a vengeance. The fresh green of the hawthorn is a sight to behold on walks and even when driving. I love to put yellow everywhere as I think of spring being the yellow time of year and a time of optimism. Crocus, daffodils, primroses, forsythia, coltsfoot, charlock and lesser celandine are just some of the flowers to be seen over March and April. Every day out walking there is something to get excited about. Changes happen rapidly and from one day to the next, we see something new.

Try to get out into the countryside. After the cold, dark winter months, we need the tonic that being out in the wildness of nature brings. In the milder, sometimes wet, spring, breathe in the earthy smells, this is particularly so in the woods and forest.

For celebration, I will decorate the house and leave offerings to Brigid on my outdoor altar. I have yellow candles lit in the house. Yellow cheers me up (as you may have guessed by now); it provides optimism, creativity, happiness, prosperity and luck.

With the warmth returning we often have a hopeful attitude to life. Spring often brings with it rejuvenation and inspiration. When the clocks change we remember whether they go back or forward by the saying, 'spring forward, fall back'. *Spring forward* is appropriate and it means progression. Our potential is unlimited and we always have room to grow. If you have been planning to do something, why not put it into action. If you are always saying that 'at the right time' you will do this and that, well you might find that you have been saying this for a long time, as the 'right time' never seems to come. So make the right time now.

On the Spring Equinox and again as with every Celtic festival, I make a special altar. Still with yellow dominating, I have yellow candles but also orange candles for overall success, happiness, motivation and creativity. Daffodils are still a favorite flower, but primroses, and any other bright spring flower are added to the altar. Hares, lambs, chicks and baby animals in general either pictures or ornaments help to remind us of the growing fertility around us. If people come to my ritual then I ask them to bring something for the altar that reminds them of the season.

This ritual follows the Imbolg ritual with the altar facing east, and the addition of asking for inspiration and motivation to carry out the projects and plans that I have already begun.

Bealtaine

At Bealtaine, the third fertility festival, for the final time I honor the growing fertility of the land and during the following summer months it also celebrates the fertility of the goddess. Áine is my goddess for the late spring and summer. She is fertile and ready for her lover, so I say goodbye to her Brigid phase as summer begins to creep in and Nature will soon be in full bloom.

Áine is an Irish goddess and faery queen of Munster and is strongly connected with Limerick. Limerick is in Munster and so is County Clare where I now live. Áine is of the Tuatha Dé Danann and her hill *Cnoc Áine*, (Knockainy) is in Limerick close to Knockainy village and Lough Gur. Áine is the goddess of love and fertility and of prosperity and summer. She brings wealth with the growth of healthy crops and is a protector of cattle.

She was raped by Ailill Olum, a Munster king, but she destroyed him for his insult to her. With the rest of the Tuatha Dé Danann, she became of the *sidhe* and as goddess of sovereignty, the faery queen.

I am often invited to the celebrations of other groups at this time. I like the informal ritual that feels natural and not too practiced — one where anyone can contribute.

Often this starts by gathering in a circle and holding hands. We do not have an altar or bring altar tools. The ritual is all about nature. This ritual might take place on private land, a garden, or at a sacred well balanced on rocks in the stream or in various places above and below a well.

If you come together with others at this time, whether it is one person or several, you can plan ahead to a certain extent. Let everyone who wishes to contribute prepare something. One of our group sings, another will read poetry, another is an eloquent speaker, another might just say something that comes to heart at that moment in time. Opening and closing the ceremony with song is particularly poignant, and the whole ceremony can stir up hidden emotions.

Rituals do not have to be formal, but can be emotional, friendly, fun or spontaneous.

Outdoor altars (facing south) can be dressed with hawthorn blossom (do not bring this indoors). Ladies can wear wreaths of flowers, a maypole can be erected, and a fire (the bel fire) lit. If you jump the fire, take care and only do so if the fire is a small one and never when you are on your own. I say this having seen at least two people trip and fall, luckily people were at hand to whisk them up before harm was done.

At this time of year, most of the leaves are out on the trees, and in the coming week or so, all of them. The whitethorn (hawthorn) is or soon will be in blossom. Up until this time I carefully watch the trees as the leaves appearing brings me great joy as I see the season change before me and everything comes alive. The air is warmer and as we shed our coats, there is an air of freedom and recklessness about.

This is a good time to organize your garden, to plant out so to enjoy the fruits of your labor in later months. If plants are too costly, you can buy packets of seeds for a fraction of the price. Spread mixed flowers liberally to produce a cottage garden.

Sowing seeds is a good theme for Bealtaine, whether this is making love, working hard at relationships, planning a marriage, trying for a baby, or as simple as actually sowing seeds for vegetables to sustain you or for flowers to add beauty to your garden.

If you have not begun any projects, you have a chance now to sow seeds for them. We cannot achieve without first making the effort. Sowing seeds now, will bring us a bountiful harvest in the future. Whether this is applying for that course at college or university, starting off your own business in a small way, looking for a new job, making changes in your relationship or home life or putting the house up for sale, you need to start from the bottom, prepare the way, sow the seeds and watch the slow growth until you can reap the harvest of your hard work. Little acorns grow into great oak trees.

To sow seeds you first need to have trust in yourself. You have to believe that you are capable of making change or building on a project. If you do not trust yourself then you will be wary of others, and they will have no faith in you. Build up positivity as it is a powerful tool. Everyone has talents and gifts albeit in different ways. You too have talents and gifts, and you can use them to build. Positive energy will help you in this.

If you are a person who puts up walls around yourself, then it is time to make an opening, or break down that wall and let people in. If you have been hurt or wronged and feel a sense of worthlessness or if you have made major mistakes, then you need to spot this and convince yourself that you are worthy. Everyone makes mistakes; no one is immune to hurt. Someone else's decision to change their life which in turn changes yours too, is not your fault. However, this does mean that you have to begin again on your own, rather than sit and wish for something to change it for you.

Accordingly, start to sow those seeds, use this time of great fertility to give you the courage to grow and progress.

The Summer Solstice

At this time Áine and Ireland is in the full bloom of midsummer. It comes naturally to me to equate midsummer with Áine, goddess and queen of faeries. For me also she is the young mother, fierce and protective.

Faeries, little people, wee folk, nature spirits have been on the earth as long if not longer than we have. I believe that they are more than one race of beings who reside in a world parallel to, almost within, our own. Faeries for sure inhabit inner space just as aliens are said to inhabit outer space.

Since this inner realm is so close to us, sometimes the veil is thin and faeries appear in our own world, especially at certain times of the day and year. These times are 'tween times' such as twilight, just before sun up and sun down, and often those times around noon and midnight twixt morning and afternoon and one day and another, and there are those times of the year such as midsummer night and Samhain (the pagan new year).

When talking to an Irish friend about faeries, we were discussing why people did not see faeries as much as they did fifty years ago. The faeries would for instance knock on a door of a house and the occupier would open it to allow the faery to walk through. People would also often just leave their doors open to allow the faeries to walk freely through the house. My friend believed that the Bean Sidhe is not heard so much either.

A friend of his many years ago was telling the story of how he had been building a house, and yet did not progress. After a week of work, there was no more work done than there had been on the first day. Then he discovered that he was building on a faery fort and stopped even trying. More recently, a local motorway was diverted around a lone faery whitethorn tree, as none of the workers would cut it down for fear of bad luck. This was later vandalized, but grew back and can still be seen.

One of the logical reasons for fewer sightings, which cropped up in the discussion, was the fact that people no longer walk over the land at night to reach their homes. Nowadays cars or taxis are used at night. Another reason was people are more wary about reporting sightings for fear of ridicule in these modern times.

Another thought was that people are perhaps no longer faery aware. In the time of the Celtic Tiger, many homes had been built with perhaps not so much thought given for faery paths, forts and trees. Together with the fear of ridicule, increase in traffic, fewer stories passed down, belief dismissed as superstition and so forth, this encouraged the faery folk to withdraw from our world. Faeries are less accepted, the environment is more hostile for them, courteousness and consideration no longer given, so who could blame them for retreating more into their own world as ours became unsympathetic. There are still sightings, but far fewer. The faery folk do not so readily mix.

There are those who are gifted with a third eye that see faeries easier than others, just as some people see spirits and some do not, even though they can be in the same room together. We can heighten are intuitiveness and enhance our psychic abilities though with practice. We all have some psychic ability; it may just be that it is different from that of our friend, brother or neighbor.

The first time I saw something strange was near our farmhouse in the west of Ireland. I had been walking up the lane with my husband when I saw something dark in the hedgerow. It was too slim to be a bird yet too big to be a dragonfly. My husband could not see it. As we came near, it suddenly disappeared. Since then I have seen other similar beings. Again, they were dark and moved rather quickly. They were first in my bedroom, and I could see something about eight inches tall swooping around me. It worried me slightly that it was a dark figure. The next time I saw them was in the living room. The room had a high thirty-foot vaulted ceiling. Half way up I could see three dark figures flying rapidly around. Again, they were about eight inches high. I did see, however, that it was only because they moved so fast combined with their clothing, which was earthy colored dark green and brown, that they appeared so dark. I did not see any wings.

So for the summer solstice we can connect with the faeries. When you are out in the garden or in nature, mentally speak with the faery folk. Make some wishes; be positive in your thoughts. Thank Áine the queen of faeries for all the good things past wishes have brought.

Midsummer is a joyous time. Outdoor ceremonies are more probable. What better than to put fresh garlands around your hair, whether you are male or female. Honor the faery folk by leaving out gifts. Dance, sing and make merry. Yes, the neighbors will think you mad, but who cares, this is a time of (excuse the adjective) devil-may-care but wholesome attitudes.

More often associated with Bealtaine, the Green Man represents the cycle of birth, life, death and rebirth. In midsummer, we celebrate life. In honor of the Green Man, your hair and neck garlands can be made of oak, whitethorn and ivy.

Lughnasadh

At the first and second harvests at Lughnasadh and throughout the autumn months I connect with the mature mother Danu, saying goodbye to the young mother Áine. Danu is the goddess of the light and the coming dark. I see her at the end of her fertility crossing over into her autumn years.

Once a high priestess and writer spoke to us — a group of friends — about the crone stage of life. We had been discussing that some of us were approaching cronehood, while others like myself were already considered crones having achieved menopause. The high priestess mentioned the views that some women held in that they considered there were four rather than three phases of life, rightly pointing out that the moon has four faces, not three. In modern tradition, the waxing moon is maidenhood, the full moon is motherhood, and the waning moon is the crone. Yet the crone she explained, living the winter months of her life and awaiting her death, does not describe the modern woman in her late forties, fifties or even sixties, who is often entering the prime of her life and is typically at her most creative.

The high priestess explained that the phase missed out is the new moon or dark phase equated with death and rebirth. Hence missing from the three stages of womanhood, maiden, mother and crone, there is a stage missing — the *autumn* of life. In the three-phase 'system' we move from motherhood to old age without any transitional phase. The high priestess told how the postmenopausal woman is lost in an 'archetype-less limbo'.

In this way, we can see the Earth Mother as four-fold: the *maiden* is the waxing moon — the spring of life; the *mother* is the full moon — the summer of life; the post-menopausal woman or *harvest queen* is the waning moon — the autumn of life; and the *crone* is the dark moon — the winter of life. Within modern paganism, there are four seasons of the year, four phases of the moon, four phases of a woman's life, four basic elements — earth, air, fire and water, and four directions — north, south, east and west, so this makes sense. Yes, there are many important and magical threes too, but here I highlight the fours.

So here, we celebrate the time of the peri-menopausal and menopausal woman, but also the mid-life of the male who also believes his life is far from over.

Therefore, this festival brings with it an awareness that soon all growth will slow down and stop, but at the same time we celebrate the bringing in of the first harvest, which will sustain us through the winter months.

So celebrate this time by honoring Danu (or your chosen goddess). Of course, with this being the celebration of Lughnasadh the god Lugh is also honored. Thank the goddess as the Earth Mother and Lugh as the master of arts and crafts, by feasting on the ripened fruits, vegetables and grains. Make a corn dolly (from the stalks of any harvested grain). Keep it until Bealtaine and then burn on the bel-fire. If you have a craft, such as metal work, jewelry, woodwork, pottery, needlecrafts, weaving or glass blowing, display your work for all to see. This is a good time with the autumn approaching to take up a craft.

The Autumn Equinox

At this time of year, all growth has stopped as we move into autumn. Danu is still my goddess, but she is now older and wiser, and about to become a grandmother.

Often a slight chill in the mornings gives us the nostalgic autumnal feeling. The leaves are already turning and the second harvest is in, or ready to bring in, for which we give hearty thanks. Depending on how good or bad summer has been we will soon be able to or already have harvested black-berries, rosehips, sloe berries, hazelnuts, elderberries, apples, damsons and fuchsia berries. September can be a busy time making syrups, wines and jams. Use these in your celebra-tions.

Celebrate the changing season by filling your altar or Craft table with fruits of the second harvest, a white and black candle and early fallen leaves of brilliant reds, bronzes and yellows.

If you are in your mid-fifties to seventy, you may be in your autumn years but you are also more wise, often embarking on a new project, business, educational course, hobby or relationship, life is far from over and can be every bit as busy as when you were younger. There is life in the old dog yet. At the same time, you may also think it is time to start winding down, taking more time out for yourself now that the family has grown or you have retired. Whichever way you go, there is a good future ahead, an Indian summer.

For all of us, this is a time of the balance between dark and light and although we may have darker evenings drawing nigh, but we can take time out to plan what we will fill our time with in the winter months and make preparations.

Rituals can be cheerful, and held outdoors as the weather is mostly still clement. Make this a time for feasting on homemade goodies.

3

Earthy Matters

Being Aware of the Elements

Being aware of the elements can help you connect with nature. Learn to be sentient to each by tuning into just one of them each day. If it is a windy day, choose that one to tune into air. If it is winter or perhaps a chilly autumn or spring evening, then light a fire and choose this time to tune into it. Water can be tuned into any time of year as we can wait for rain, or go to the ocean, or a river or well. Earth can be connected to by walking, running or dancing on it, or simply tidying your garden or planting your shrubs and flowers.

The Magic of Water

Water connects to the west and is wonderful, an essential ingredient for life and covers one third of our world. As we are also made up mainly of water, it is not surprising how we are often so drawn to it, be it the smallest stream or the largest ocean. Water keeps us alive and cleanses us. Water refreshes the dry earth so our crops can grow. We use water for washing our vegetables, for cooking, and we water our gardens with it. We use it as a source of power. Water can be calming, terrifying and destructive and is emotion and feelings. As with any body of water, at times, it flows fast and furious as our passions do, or it is passive as our empathy is or rocky as can be our relationships. In magic, we might mix it with salt to mark out the boundary of our circle and we use it to cleanse our crystals. These are only some of the uses of water both practical and magical.

I used to live close to a river (I now look over a huge lake).

When I was out walking, I would walk over the bridge of the river and on up the hill to look over a lake. If I walked a little further I came upon a waterfall. Behind my home were two sacred wells and there are many more in that area. At the time I lived there, there was flooding after heavy rain. On the one hand, the water flooded people's homes, destroying their belongings and even causing some people to have to be rescued, but on the other hand, the river that usually gently meandered along was magnificent as a raging torrent, and the local waterfalls were beautiful in their full flow.

Water can be used to say goodbye to someone who has passed on. I have had two people in recent years who were important in my life, and passed away far too young and when they had so much more to give. I was unable to attend the funeral of either one. Instead, in both cases I went to a local river and held my own little ritual for them. After thinking of the person and talking to them, I said my goodbyes and told them how they touched my life and that I would never forget them. I finished by throwing some flowers into the flowing water and watched them float away.

When we are in need of healing, water can help us. When we are in need of cleansing away negative events in our lives (or the leftovers of them), then water can help us. Have you ever experienced a good feeling from dangling your feet in a stream or brook? Most of us have. After a bath, do you have a feeling of freshness, relaxation and are more ready to face the world? Again, most of us have.

When you have negative thoughts, you can go to a body of water, be it an ocean, river or brook, to think of certain words such as 'guilt' or 'anger' and mentally throw them into the water. Watch them be carried away.

When you are in need of psychological healing, say after a broken relationship, then take a cleansing bath. Add sea salt to the warm water and cleansing herbs (in a bag) or oils if you wish, and wash away all of the negative residue. After you have finished, let the water drain away and the negativity with it. Otherwise take a shower and rub yourself with handfuls of salt and rinse it away.

Sacred wells are special places to ask for healing for yourself and others. If you are lucky enough to have one close to you, then go to it. Tie rags or ribbons of natural material to the trees close to the well in the age-old tradition. Make wishes as you tie them on. Wash your face and hands in the water of the well. If it is safe to do so, drink some of the water. Stand at the well for a while contemplating on your wishes.

The Magic of Earth

Earth connects to the north and is what we walk upon every day, solid beneath our feet — it is our world. Earth is life, birth, death and rebirth. Earth is fertile and nurturing and in this aspect, we often call her Mother Earth. The earth is the real world, the practical world. Every time we walk, we physically connect with the earth even though we do not actually think of it as such. If you love gardening you connect with the earth, in fact this is a good way to do so. We ground ourselves by deeply connecting ourselves to the earth. The earth is from which we grow and gather the harvest. We make our homes upon the earth, often buying land to add to our own homestead or estate, no matter how small or large it is. The earth is the physical, solid and practical side to our world.

Most of us feel foolish to be seen doing something perhaps only children or drunken people would do. We might be a very dignified person that avoids looking silly. In doing this we also lose our sense of freedom. Go and dance in the rain and run barefoot through a meadow. If you have a problem with this kind of freedom, then put on waterproof clothes and waterproof boots and you will soon find yourself jumping in puddles. Dance outside with your animal guide or in the garden. If you have a problem with this, then do it at night. Does it really matter if you are caught hugging a tree or dancing around it?

Shuffle through the fallen leaves of autumn.

Find some pens or paints, paper or canvas, and sit outside. Draw what comes into your head. It does not matter if you are artistic or not, just let your imagination flow and do not worry about the finished product.

Make a collage of cuttings you find in magazines and add something of nature to it.

If you do not already do this, then collect objects from nature, a fir cone, a pretty pebble or shell, a feather, leaf, small branch, bark, or a twig. You can also make a special table for them.

Perhaps you prefer going to the beach and making a sand sculpture or simple sand pies.

The Magic of Fire

Fire is connected to the south. Fire is beauty, energy, excitement, inspiration, creativity, enthusiasm and passion. Fire can destroy but in doing so purifies. Fire keeps us warm in the cold winter months and we use fire to cook on and light our way in actuality and symbolically. Where fire has raged, new growth appears. As the sun, it is the giver of life. We plant our crops in the earth, the water feeds them, and the sun warms them.

There is nothing like an open fire that we can gather around in the spirit of comradeship. We can divine the future by staring into the flames and reading the pictures we see there.

Fire is spiritual and magical. We light candles for spell work and the flame helps the spell vibrations go out into the universe. When we want to be calm, we use candlelight for ambience. We might light candles when we pray or to help a spirit on its journey into the next world.

Fire is rebirth. Have you often thought a fire was out only for it to spring to life again? The phoenix rises from the flames, immortal and renewed and goes on to live again until once more it dies and is reborn. This is life. We often have periods in our lives that have to die, sometimes this is not of our own making, but we are reborn, we reinvent ourselves and begin a new phase in our lives, until again in time that phase might also die. This is the magic of fire, the energy and passion to start and to grow again.

If you find yourself at the end of a phase of your life, perhaps because of divorce, the death of a partner, or the end of a career, you can call on fire to provide the energy you need move on or start again. Go out in the sun and reach your face up and feel the warmth on your skin. Let it revitalize you. Keep candles lit or a hearth fire while you reassess your life, ask for inspiration and formulate new plans.

If you are feeling low, why not invite some friends around. Light a fire indoors or out and sit around in the spirit of comradeship. As we talk, tell stories, eat and drink together we feel comforted and strengthened. Often when we do this if we attend an event, it is the one thing everyone talks about after, so why not do it more often.

When you have lost your way, symbolically use a lamp, torch or candle to show you the way again. Meditate on the light and search for the answers.

The Magic of Air
Air is connected with the east and is the breath of life and is changeable, calm, ferocious, communicative, intellectual, associated with memory and logic and perhaps more significantly is spiritual. We cannot see air, we can only feel it. This gives it a spiritual quality. Air is unpredictable in that it is the

wind that blows a gentle breeze or a terrible hurricane. Air is connected with the intellect, memory and logic. Changeable, air can also be dreaming.

Air takes away the last of the leaves from the trees in autumn and winter to prepare them for new growth. Air carries the seeds to propagate the earth. We go out in the fresh air to clear our heads so we can think more clearly. We go to the countryside to breathe the clean air to cleanse our bodies. Air is the sky, a deep azure blue. When we float on the air in astral projection, we can travel into the atmosphere and see for ourselves that the sky is not a roof, and we can go beyond it to the stars.

For moments of calm during a stormy time in your life, lie on your back on the ground and look at the sky. Watch the airflow push the clouds along. You can read (or scry) the cumulous clouds, or look for sylphs when the sky is brightest blue with just the thin cirrus wisps. Alternatively, if this is not possible, light white and yellow candles. The flame is fanned and kept alive by air.

When you are out on a bright spring day, feel the breeze toying with your hair. Breathe it in expanding your lungs and clearing your head.

On a gusty day go out and collect windfall wands or items for your altar or nature table and watch as the sycamore seed spins to the ground. In autumn, watch the leaves fall down like golden rain.

People who have too much air tend to be dreamy. In this case, bring some earth in to join the air, in the form of green or brown candles, or ground yourself. Let air's logic feed through to you by mixing talking with your thinking. It helps sometimes to talk with others to help reason things out. If you need some direction, try to do something creative such as writing poetry or intellectual by taking up some study.

The Land, Sea and Sky

Being interested and also connected with all things Celtic, I do also work with the land, sea and sky. However, this is in my own way. For instance, I see each of these as realms and connected with the otherworld. Close to my home, I can see all three, the land, sea or water and the sky, as many of us can. The realms are there for us to easily connect with as we come across them daily. We do tend to take them for granted. How often do you look up and study the sky, or dangle your feet in the water or watch the waves crash onto the shore, or just run barefoot across a meadow or just stand and study and take it all in? To really connect we need to do this often.

Land

For me the land is the ground we walk upon, the earth beneath my feet, the trees, plants and people. I regularly walk in the lanes, forests and fields surrounding my home. The land is connected with the realms of the otherworld. I cross the hedge from this world to the otherworld by hedge riding. I never know what I will see there; sometimes it is humans and often faery folk. I cross the landscape of the otherworld by walking or by riding one of my animal guides (a white ox and a white horse). There are a host of different earth spirits, such as gnomes, elves, leprechauns and dwarves to meet there. Still, there is nothing like just walking on the land in reality and connecting with the earth beneath us.

Sea

The sea is mystical and magical and has much power. It is uncontrollable, magnificent, calm or stormy and beneath it lay many secrets. The sea is so deep there are many things we do not know about it and creatures we have never seen.

To connect with the spiritual creatures of the sea, I go to it or a connecting body of water such as a river and speak with the water spirits who might be merpeople, selkies or merrows. I might paddle in the sea or walk along the beach, or sit and watch the stream wind its way down into the valley.

In an otherworld journey, I can swim in the water and connect directly with the spirits of the water, often for healing or cleansing purposes.

Sky

The sky stretches above us. In the day, it can be a variety of wonderful colors, azure, grey, dark gray, yellow and orange, and has the rainbow, which spans the sky with its seven colors. There are many different cloud formations, which can be magnificent. At night, especially here in Ireland with less light pollution, the whole sky is covered with millions of stars and sparkles like lights on a Yule tree.

Many gods and goddesses are of the sky as are sylphs who soar among the cirrus clouds.

I connect with the sky during astral travel and hedge riding. I fly across the sky, way above the ground, and sometimes far up into the atmosphere.

4

Sacred Trees

All trees are sacred, but there are certain trees that are sacred to different religions, spiritual paths and mythologies. The tree is symbolic of the three realms as the roots reach deep into the ground, the trunk is of the land often edging water and the branches reach into the sky. Below are my own favorite sacred trees, with which I work.

The Magical Triad

Oak Tree — Strength
The oak tree is perhaps the most revered tree of all and is known as the 'Father of the Woods'. It was not just the Druids and Celts that held this tree sacred, but also the Greek, Roman and Teutonic peoples.

The Druids are thought to have worshipped the oak in groves and modern Druids still do. Mistletoe, also a sacred plant of the Druids, can occasionally be entwined in the oak's branches. The oak represents strength and endurance yet it is struck by lightning more than any other tree, most probably owing to low electrical resistance. Accordingly, it is not surprising that it is associated with the element *fire*.

In Norse mythology, the oak is the tree of Thor the god of thunder, lightning and storms, and protector of humankind. Thor represents all the attributes of the oak, of strength, valiance, courage and protector against the forces of evil. Zeus was the Greek chief of gods and was also the god of an oracle established at an oak tree (although sometimes this is the beech) at Dodona in Greece.

There is an old folk rhyme, which talks of *turning your cloak* because *faery folks are in old oaks.* Turning your outer clothing such as your jacket or cloak, would protect you from the faeries, especially if you were traveling in remote areas.

The oak is the tree of the dryad, a female nymph-like nature spirit. The dryad inhabits the oak tree and blends in with it, as she is shy. She usually stays within sight of her tree, and will rarely move more than three hundred yards from it. The dryad stays with the tree for life and dies with it, so can live for centuries.

The Oakmen are strange dwarf-like creatures. They are ugly like most dwarfs and act as guardians of the oak and oak groves. They are said to wear red caps and like many faery folk, they are reclusive or shy, but are not harmful.

The oak appears in the mythology of many peoples, and is one of the trees which has an affinity with the goddess (also saint) Brigid.

The oak can be counted among the most sacred of faery trees for contact with faery and is one of the triad of faery trees, the other two being hawthorn and ash.

Ash Tree — Life

The ash tree grows tall into the heavens. Like the oak, it is prone to be struck by lightning. The ash tree is well known over centuries for its healing energies. Most often, this was connected with babies and young children, but also with animals.

The ash is known to have been used in magic, especially for wands and staffs. Gwydion the magician, who appears in Celtic mythology in the fourth branch of the Mabinogi, is said to have fashioned his wands from ash, although he did not always put them to good use. There is also some protection afforded against enchantment if a person carried ash keys.

Yggdrasil is the World Tree and is thought to be a gigantic ash tree. Odin the All-Father hung from Yggdrasil in a self-sacrificing ritual in search of enlightenment. He took up the runes lying beneath and gained the wisdom and knowledge of them.

The ash tree provides us with healing. It also offers us enlightenment often through self-sacrifice, which can mean giving more and taking less. This does not mean just in a material way, but in other ways, such as giving our time by lending a sympathetic ear, and offering help to those in need.

Dryads or wood nymphs are attached to the ash tree, and these particular ones are the Meliae. The Meliae are daughters of Gaia or Mother Earth and have been linked with the fates and honey-nymphs. The Meliae ash-tree sisters nursed Zeus as a baby and occasionally accompany Pan the Horned God of the forest.

If there is a blockage in your life, there is hope for the future. This is where the spiritual side of you comes into effect. Go to the ash tree for guidance. It will help you dig deep within you to see further into your life and gain some well needed optimism.

Hawthorn Tree — Faery Tree

There are other names for the hawthorn and it is known in Ireland as the whitethorn but has other names such as mayflower or mayblossom. My mother used to call it the 'bread and cheese tree' and she and her brothers and sisters would eat the young buds and leaves from it on the way to school on the Isle of Man. She would never bring the blossom into the house, as it was unlucky to do so.

Lone trees or groves of three or more trees are said to be the most magical. Although known for its *mayblossom*, nowadays the hawthorn blossoms in April or May and occasionally in March. What is now known as The

Glastonbury Thorn grows in the abbey grounds there, the original was said to have been planted by Joseph of Arimathea. This thorn tree is unusual as it flowers twice in the year at yuletide and in the spring. The original was cut down in the English Civil War, but the abbey thorn and other hawthorn trees exist at Glastonbury, which are thought to be cuttings of the original tree.

The hawthorn is one of the trees of the witch. As such, it is usual that the witch uses it for magical purposes.

As it is a thorn tree, it is protective. For me it is the tree of the faery. As one of the portal triad of trees with oak and ash, I go to this tree the most to greet the faery folk.

The hawthorn is used by pagans on Bealtaine. If they are lucky enough to find the tree in blossom, it is used for garlands or on outdoor altars. Placing it over doorways brings protection. However, when cutting, avoid lone trees and always leave a gift both to the tree itself and to the faeries of the tree.

As faeries inhabit the tree, it is said to be unlucky to cut it down or dig it up. In Ireland, there are tales of lone hawthorn trees bleeding or bad luck coming to the folk who destroy them. Roads are generally directed around them and farmers cultivate around them.

Other Magical Trees

Apple Tree — Love

The ancient apple tree can be both wild and cultivated with a variety of flavors from the sour crab and cooking apples to the dessert apples with many other apple tastes in between. In the spring, the fragrant blossom fills the trees. The world would be a sadder place without the humble, but noble apple. Many traditional customs involve the apple. Sadly, not as many people follow these customs now. The apple is very much connected with the Celtic festival Samhain and many customs accompany the fruit for this day.

The apple tree is a magical tree connected to the other-world and appears more frequently in folklore than perhaps any other tree, often taking an important part. Avalon is 'The Isle of Apples'.

The apple is the fruit of the otherworld. One was given to Thomas the Rhymer by the Queen of Elfland and this gave him the gift of prophecy and a tongue that never lied.

There is a Celtic myth associated with the apple. In this tale, a strange faery maiden appears to *Connla*, the son of *Conn* of the hundred fights (or battles) and only he can see her. She tells him she comes from a faery mound and is in love with him and wishes to take him back with her. Hearing this, Conn the king wanting to prevent it, asks for help from his Druid counsel who makes a charm. The charm causes the faery maiden to disappear, but before doing so, she throws Connla a magic apple. For a whole month, the apple is all Connla can eat or wishes to eat as he so longs for the maiden. At last, she returns and they sail away together and are never seen again.

As you can see, the apple appears to be used as an enchantment often connected with love.

So in love matters, be careful what you wish for or you might just get it and are unable to rid yourself of it so easily. For help go to the tree itself and ask for solutions to problems to come to you.

Aspen Tree — Astral Travel and Voice

The graceful aspen tree is famous for its quivering or trembling leaves, even when all other trees are still. As it does so, it whispers. The aspen is a unisexual tree and has a pale gray slender trunk, its leaves bud first as copper, turning to bright green in the summer and to gold or bright yellow in the winter.

Its wood was used as a defensive shield. This is a defense against psychic as well as physical harm. The aspen is a tree favored by animals as fodder; among them are the deer, goat and sheep.

The aspen belongs to the poplar family and is a tree of the spirit. In medieval times, the poplar bud or leaf was used in flying ointment. This means it provides passage into the otherworld in a shamanistic way or by astral travel. It allows the user to come and go safely.

The aspen talks to us as we pass by and we look up and take notice. When you need the gift of voice, go to this tree and listen to what it tells you.

I try to keep a sprig of this on my altar and keep it by me when travelling to the otherworld.

Birch Tree — New Beginnings
In his poem, *The Picture or The Lover's Resolution*, the poet Samuel Taylor Coleridge named the birch tree the *Most beautiful of forest trees, the Lady of the Woods*. The weeping branches of the silver birch droop gracefully and the dazzling silver white bark indeed makes this a beautiful tree to behold.

Witches use birch besoms for rituals and for flights. The brush is the birch twigs tied with willow strips and the handle is of ash wood. Birch was and still is used to sweep out the Celtic old year at Samhain and is connected to the fertility festival Bealtaine. As this tree is related to fertility and children, it is a tree of new beginnings as indicated in Berkano the birch, a rune of the Elder Futhark. Cradles and baby toys are often made with birch as it has protective qualities especially where children are concerned. The traditional maypole, a fertility symbol, is made of birch and therefore has a great connection with the festival Bealtaine.

The Scottish tree-dweller the Gille Dubh or Ghillie Dhu preferred the birch or birch thickets. He is a strange character with wild black hair and clothes woven of leaves and moss. He is reclusive but is also known to be compassionate, especially towards children.

The birch is high up on my list of favorites. Most people often require new starts in many different areas of their lives and I am no exception. I hardly ever walk past a birch without stopping and paying homage. I sometimes ask the tree for help with a new beginning and always have birch twigs and branches on my altar.

Blackthorn Tree — Protection

The blackthorn tree is thornier than the hawthorn. And while the hawthorn is a tree which brings luck, the blackthorn has more negative connotations. The branches are dense and it makes a good hedge of protection to guard boundaries of property. The flowers appear first with this tree bringing beauty to the dark winter. The wood has been used for many things including the Irish shillelagh and magic wands, making it a magical tree. The blackthorn fruit (the sloe) is used in cooking and to make sloe gin.

As a *black* thorn, this tree does have undertones of absorbance and the dispersing of negative energy. The blackthorn is said to be representative of the waning moon and year but when the first signs of spring appear, blackthorn is there to brighten us with its blossom, suggesting it is more representative of the waning moon and waning year leading up to the New Moon and spring.

The Irish tribe of faeries the Lunantishee guard the blackthorn, and it is unlucky to cut a branch from it on either May 11th or November 11th. If you do so, misfortune will ensue.

When you need protection then go to the blackthorn and ask for it.

Elder Tree — Protection, Abundance

The elder tree has long been used as a protector of homes and animals. It wards away evil spirits and negative energy. Witches are said to be able to turn themselves into elder trees. The Rollright Stones, an ancient stone circle in Oxfordshire, England, have the legend of a king who tried to conquer England and was turned into a stone by a witch (The King Stone), along with his men (The King's Men Stones), and his knights (The Whispering Knights). The witch turned herself into an elder tree. Faeries are said to live beneath the Rollright Stones and come out at midnight to joyfully dance around them in the moonlight. If the tree is cut while in blossom, rather like the hawthorn, it is said to bleed.

The elder tree gives beautiful pungent white blossom and delicious fruit, which has long been used in remedies and wine making. The blossom has a narcotic scent and musical instruments are made from its wood.

The Hyldemoer or Elder Mother inhabits the tree and is a friendly soul but can be tricky especially if you harm her tree. Take care if you cut down an elder for the wood, especially for making cradles, as Hyldemoer will haunt your house and torment your baby. Ask permission of her first for using the wood for any other purpose. Cutting down this tree as with the hawthorn is said to be unwise.

Hazel — Wisdom

The hazel tree was sacred to the Druids, and lies at the heart of the otherworld. The tree is occasionally to be found near holy wells. The hazel resembles a shrub more than a tree, but it does appear occasionally with a single trunk and it thrives in damp places. The fruit of the hazel is known by all, and its pliable wood has many uses including walking sticks, staffs and hoops. Rods of hazel are used to dowse for water. A Y-shaped branch is cut and used to make natural handles.

When the point twitches, water, energy or minerals can be found.

The hazel tree grows near to Connla's Well (this is a second Connla of Celtic mythology), which lies under the sea in the *Land of Youth*. The fruit and blossom of wisdom, knowledge and inspiration, fall into the well causing a flow of purple onto the water. Salmon chew on the fruit and take on the color, which gives them speckles. The well and the water in it, the salmon and the hazel, all together make a magical combination. The faery goddess Sinann, daughter of Lir the great sea god, went to the well and it appears was either not permitted to do so, or omitted to perform certain ceremony, resulting in the angry water washing her away towards the ocean. Her body came to rest on the shore of a river, which from thence on was named the Shannon, after her. The River Shannon lies in Ireland.

Nine hazel trees also grow close to the magical well of wisdom called Segais. Again, the hazel fruit falls into the water and is eaten by the salmon. This time it is Boann, meaning 'White Cow', the wife of Nechtan (although some sources give other names), who was the lover of the Dagda with whom she had a son. Her husband was guardian of the well. In this case Boann did not follow the protocol of the well, and walked around it widdershins. Like Sinann she was swept away by a surge of water losing or injuring an arm, a leg and an eye, and eventually her life. The resulting river, the Boyne, was named after her. The River Boyne runs close to a cluster of sidhe mounds in Ireland, including Newgrange.

The hazel appears in many superstitions regarding divining, you throw two nuts into the fire if you are trying to choose between lovers. The first one to crack is the true one. You can also throw two nuts in the fire to represent you and your lover, if they burn long and slow together, you will be happy. If one nut jumps apart from the other, you will not.

The cobnut comes from the family of hazel. You have to be quick to beat the squirrels to the nuts. For wisdom and knowledge, I usually have a few hazel or cobnuts on my desk or altar.

Holly Tree — Recharging
Holly is the tree we love to have in our homes at Yuletide to celebrate the return of the light. Its dark green shiny leaves and bright red berries symbolize fertility within the barren winter, not least that it cheers us with its beauty and color. Holly brings eternal hope, growth and renewal.

The holly is another protective tree and was said to repel magic, to drain opponents of their strength and protect homes from lightning. Only the female tree produces the cheerful red berries though both the male and female tree produce fragrant white blossom in early summer. At Yuletide, the holly is often coupled with the ivy.

The holly is a tree of Danu who is the mother of the Tuatha Dé Danann. She is goddess and faery queen and my goddess of late summer and autumn. The Danube is said to have been named after her. Not much is known about her but she is the goddess of the faery people and the fertile land. She is also sometimes said to be the mother of the Dagda whom she begot with the oak tree *Bile* after watering it.

Rowan Tree — Protection
The rowan tree is also called the Mountain Ash even though it is not a member of the ash family and is a favorite tree of the Scottish highlands. The rowan has clusters of fragrant creamy-white blossom in spring and lovely red berries in the autumn, though they never last long as they are a huge attraction for the birds. The berries are edible but taste rather bitter and are more often used in jams. The rowan is one of autumn's most colorful trees with pink, gold and scarlet

leaves. As it is a strong wood, over the centuries, rowan has been used to make spinning wheels, spindles and walking sticks.

Although many trees have protective qualities, the rowan tree is perhaps the most protective of all and is foremost in protection against negative influences. At the stalk end of the berries, you will see a tiny five-pointed star or pentagram, a magical and ancient symbol of protection. The rowan has protected homes for centuries.

The rowan is yet another tree sacred to Brigid of the Tuatha Dé Danann, patron of crafts and spinning. Her fiery arrows are also said to have been made from rowan wood.

In the following tale as with all mythology, there are various spellings of the names of the characters involved. Deep in the Forest of Dooras there was a Fomorian one-eyed giant, protector of the rowan or quicken tree of immortality, called Searbhan the Surly One. He guarded the tree for the faery tribe of Tuatha Dé Danann. The tree had grown from a berry, which came from faeryland having been accidentally dropped by the faery folk. It was indeed a magical tree. A runaway couple Diarmuid and Grainne came upon the tree while being pursued by Fionn who was Grainne's spurned husband to be. Grainne requested berries from the tree, which were said to taste as sweet as honey. After a battle, Searbhan was slain by Diarmuid with three strikes of his own iron club. Diarmuid was then able to obtain the berries for his love, Grainne.

Each year I take a few sprigs of rowan with berries and keep them on my altar to use in protection spells.

Spindle Tree — Industry
There is something really magical about this tree when the scarlet buds appear in late summer. I am drawn to it. While on a visit to my daughter's home, I took a walk and my eyes

suddenly looked to the left and I was delighted to see this tree. I stood for a while and was reluctant to move onwards. On the way back, I missed the tree but came to a fork in the path. I was torn between choosing which one to take. I suddenly felt propelled towards one path, and it was not the one I had come along on the way. As soon as I stepped on it, I saw three spindle trees. Again I had been drawn towards them.

The spindle tree often grows in the hedgerows. A small but very useful tree, the wood has been used for centuries in the making of spindles. The wood is also excellent for making artists' charcoal, and the seeds make a yellow dye. In the waning year it is a beautiful sight of crimson leaves (changing from its mid-green), with rose red or bright pink fruits with orange seeds. However, the scent from the tree is not pleasant and its fruits are poisonous.

Frau Holda (Holle, Huldra) is the faery patron of spinning and weaving. She is the good Faery Godmother's equivalent. She regularly appears during the twelve days of Christmas. She rewards hard work and industry. As many faery queens do, she can appear in two forms, one an old woman with crooked teeth and nose, and one a beautiful young woman all dressed in white.

I sometimes keep a sprig of the spindle on my desk to encourage me to work harder, and hard work brings good rewards.

Willow Tree — Healing
The willow tree is the most beautiful and graceful of trees, especially the weeping willow, and is a sacred Druid tree. The old Irish name for it is Saille, though there are various spellings. Together with the ash and birch, willow is the third wood that makes up the witch's besom, its flexible branches or fronds tying the birch twigs together, while ash wood is

the handle.

The willow loves water and it is near the water you will more frequently find it growing, particularly near rivers. Willow is a tree of the moon and lunar magic. Magic wands sometimes come from the willow as one of my own does.

As one of the first trees to show sign of growth after the long winter, it is also one of the first trees I touch. There is something magical about this tree.

The willow tree is a tree of goddess, saint and faery, Brigid of the Tuatha Dé Danann, and woman of the faery hills. Brigid is a fire goddess but is also linked with water and sacred wells. She is the patron of poets and a goddess of inspiration. Brigid is a midwife and healer and her healing waters are in the wells and streams, although she has connections with rivers and lakes too. A tree of inspiration especially of poets and musicians you can go to it to enhance your creativeness.

The fronds reach down into the water and water is healing. The bark is intricate and has deep fissures. When in need of physical or mental healing, put your hands on the trunk and feel the tree's power. Absorb some of it, and remember to thank the tree after.

Yew Tree — Death and Rebirth

Though not a tall tree, the yew is strong and has an extremely long life. The oldest yew in Europe (Scotland) is thought to be 3,000 years old. All of its parts are poisonous to humans, although deer love to feed off it. Yew is the tree of immortality as it symbolizes death and rebirth. When a yew dies, new ones grow from branches that touch the ground and grow into independent trees around the old trunk. The yew has the power of renewal as new grows from the old. This beautiful evergreen tree often grows in graveyards. Yew wood was traditionally used for longbows.

This tree also has connotations of reincarnation. In the Celtic tale of the wooing of Etain, it is told of how a Druid was asked by Eochaid to find his missing wife (Etain). The Druid, by writing Oghams on four wands of yew, found her living with Midir in the faery mound or sidhe of the Bri Leith. Etain had been married to Midir in her former life, but she was killed by his first wife who had changed her into a purple fly. In trying to escape, she had eventually fallen into a drinking cup and was swallowed by the chieftain's wife Etar. The wife of Etar had then fallen pregnant and in due time gave birth once more to Etain, who reborn lived her life again not knowing anything of her previous identity.

The fire within this tree is holy, purifying and renewing. The yew signifies rebirth on a higher level and is protective. For ending something that it now dead and beginning again, you can do no better than to go to the yew tree for help regenerating.

5

Herbal Lore

As Pagans and witches, many of us have an interest in herbs. We may use herbs in healing, magic and of course cooking. Please do buy a number of books on this subject to compare and contrast as they can widely differ and also if you want to work with harvesting herbs at particular moon phases or astrologically sympathetic times.

To obtain herbs we can visit a health store perhaps, or buy online, but we can also grow our own and find wild herbs in the countryside.

Talk to your herbs when picking and using to tell them your purpose and enhance their power.

The Hedgerows

Be careful when picking wildflowers and herbs. There are many deadly plants in our hedgerows. For instance, hemlock has many look-alikes and is poisonous.

If you are picking a common herb in an unprotected area then make sure you do not take the root but only the top so it can re-grow much like the plants in your own garden.

Be careful where you pick your herbs. Leave them if they are close to a busy road or in a popular dog walking area, as they can become contaminated. Always wash wildflowers and wild herbs if you intend to consume them.

Growing Herbs

When growing your own herbs you will need a small patch in your yard/garden or a window, large pot or a series of small pots.

If you intend to grow herbs in your yard or garden, find a spot near to the house and close to a path. The reason for this is you may need to collect your herbs at night or during bad weather. You do not want to traipse through mud to get to it, or struggle down the length of the garden in the darkness. The traditional place for a herb patch is close to your kitchen, but this might not be possible as you may well have it paved in that area or it might not receive enough sun. If that is indeed the case then find another suitable but convenient place.

You may want to section off separate areas with pebbles or stones or provide separate pots for those plants that spread, such as mint, peppermint and lemon balm.

Remember to plants flowers too, such as lavender, chamomile and roses.

Harvest the herbs when they are at their best. Hang them in bunches or lay them on trays in a warm dry area. When thoroughly dry, take off the leaves and/or flowers and put them into airtight jars of dark glass, or store in a cupboard or dark area. The light can cause your herbs to deteriorate more rapidly. Replace yearly with your fresh stock.

If you have never grown herbs before, then start simply with the most well known of herbs such as parsley, sage, rosemary, thyme, mint, basil (summer months only in colder areas), bay, oregano (in colder countries shelter it in winter), lavender, chamomile (from seed), roses, and lemon balm (Melissa). You can use all these in teas, remedies, cooking or in magical practices, with many having more than one use.

You can buy pots of herbs from supermarkets and although I have heard people say they are not suitable to plant out, I have found the opposite.

Healing Herbs
Many herbs have healing abilities. For instance in my garden

I have self-heal and clover. Both of these can be used for herbal remedies. Self-heal is excellent as a gargle and antiseptic, and Red Clover is said to improve hot flushes in the menopause and also relieve congestion and as a general immune system tonic. I am not going to go into the healing properties of herbs, as everyone should check for contraindications. Herbs should be used with great care as with any medicine as they may interact with your own medications and cause problems. They may not suit you or you could be allergic to them. I would suggest going on a course of herbal medicine.

Begin simply by making natural remedies with herbs you know best and are sure of identification and possible side effects.

Magical Herbs

Herbs can be used for incenses for meditations, ritual and for magic. They can also be used as an ingredient in spells, in sachets for magic and cleansing baths and more.

Nicolas Culpeper

Dr Johnson said, 'Culpeper, the man that first ranged the woods and climbed the mountains in search of medicinal and salutary herbs, undoubtedly merited the gratitude of prosperity.'

Nicholas Culpeper a botanist and physician was at first an apprentice to an apothecary and later his wrote his *Complete Herbal* in the mid 1600s. He went out into the countryside to collect his herbs and used a combination of his knowledge of herbs with astrology to treat his patients. He was highly respected though was accused of witchcraft in the English Civil War, but eventually died of tuberculosis aged thirty-eight in 1654.

Although many of Culpeper's remedies still apply, we now have to take care and look to modern herbalists for accurate information as herbs have now been tried and tested for medical properties; Culpeper is however still useful for the astrology side of herbs and for magic. I have used his ideas for astrological properties of herbs below where they apply. Otherwise, I have used one or two of the various planets associated with that herb. In assigning an element to a herb, I have used either Culpeper or the 'nature' or basic essence of any particular herb.

Parsley

According to Culpeper, parsley is a herb of Mercury. It is also a herb of air. In this context, it is useful for communication. I add it to a selection of herbs for flying incense and it is used in flying ointments. Parsley also repels negativity and can be one of the herbs used in a cleansing bath for purification.

Sage

Culpeper says that sage is a herb of Jupiter. Some sources indicate that this herb is a plant of air or earth. It promotes healing if placed around someone who is ill. It can also be added to a sachet and put in the bed of the sufferer. Sage is a cleansing herb and therefore can be used in a purification herbal bath bundle. It has long been known to promote longevity and immortality. Use it also for psychic work and divination.

Rosemary

According to Culpeper, rosemary is a herb of the sun and of Aries the Ram and is therefore a fire plant but some sources quote this as a plant of water. Rosemary aids memory and can be used in incense. It absorbs negativity so can also be used in a sachet of cleansing herbs for baths. As a known herb in matters of the heart, Rosemary can be used for love (though putting spells of love on someone in particular is negative magic). Use sparingly.

Thyme

Culpeper tells us that thyme is a herb of Venus. This plant is also a plant of air. Use it when courage is needed. I use this in incenses for psychic work. For restful sleep and protection against nightmares, use in a sleep pillow or sachet for under the pillow, or tie to the bedstead above the bed. Thyme is also a cleansing herb.

Mint

Culpeper tells us that spearmint is a plant of Venus but also said to be a plant of Mercury and this also applies to mint. A plant of air again it is useful in psychic work. It is a herb that can uplift your spirits and I have to say that mint tea certainly does. Use it in incense.

Basil

This herb is not included in Culpeper but is a useful herb for magic. This herb is a herb of water and of Mars and is commonly used in money spells and to attract prosperity. Basil is useful as a herb of protection, and to ward off evil entities. Use also for love and faithfulness.

Bay

Culpeper tells us that bay is a tree of the sun and of the astrological sign Leo and a fiery herb. Bay is a major herb for protection and the warding away of negative witchcraft or curses. A herb of many benefits, use for attraction of wealth, for prophecy and for pleasant dreaming.

Flowers

Lavender
According to Culpeper, lavender is an herb of Mercury. I would not be without lavender as it has multiple uses. An airy plant it can be used for love, as an aphrodisiac, for calming, sleep inducing, psychic work, purification and protection. Lavender has a wonderful perfume and can be used to flavor teas and added to incense not just for the above purposes but also to improve fragrance.

Chamomile
Culpeper informs us that the Egyptians dedicated this flower to the sun. Again this fiery (but also associated with water) but calming herb is good for psychic work and for pleasant dreaming. Use also for protection and purification.

Rose
Culpeper tells us that different species of rose are ruled by various planets. Red is Jupiter, white is the moon, and Damask is Venus. The rose is also a flower of air and fire. Most roses come under the astrological sign of Libra. Damask rose is a good old-fashioned rose used in healing, cooking and to make rose water. I use rose water on my face for beauty purposes every day. I dry my own rose petals (they are very expensive to buy) and use them as follows: love attraction (red rose); luck (yellow rose); purification (white rose). Also use for protection, purification and divination.

Wildflowers

Mugwort
According to Culpeper, mugwort is a herb of Venus and of the astrological signs of Taurus and Libra. Of water, it often

grows on wasteland and near water. I used to collect mine from close to the river. The scent of the flowers is lovely even when they are dying off. One of the most magical herbs and one that I hate to be without, mugwort is a potent herb for prophecy, psychic work and to promote astral projection, hedgeriding or shamanic journeying. Mugwort is a herb of protection and can drive away evil entities. To identify it, look it up on the internet and in books on wildflowers.

Ragwort

Another wildflower I would like to include and which Culpeper says is a herb of Venus. Ragwort grows in pastures and is poisonous to cattle and other animals. You would have to consume large amounts to do you harm as would animals, but still I would not take it as a medicine. Use it for protection. It was commonly said to be used by witches to ride upon at night. I often hold a sprig when I hedge ride in a symbolic way.

Meadowsweet

Culpeper places meadowsweet or Queen of the Meadows under the ruling of Venus. This grows prolifically in the fields and meadows. I picked mine from the field attached to my home here in Ireland. Meadowsweet sweetens incenses adding a lovely fragrance. A herb that gladdens the heart, many people use it in teas. Magically and as a plant of air it is used for happiness, love and for peacemaking.

How to Dry Herbs

Collect your herbs when they are at their best, this might be when they are in bloom or before they flower. Alternatively, check on the internet when is the best time to harvest them. Shake or rinse them if they are intended for consumption then lay them on wire racks and place in a warm dry place.

Alternatively lay them on trays of paper towel and keep in a warm and dry place. You can also hang them in bunches from racks or hooks. When they have thoroughly dried out, break them up and place in jars and seal. They need to be kept in a cool dark place.

6

Folk Magic

The ingredients of my spells more often than not are collected from the wild. Sometimes I store items such as rowanberries for use in the winter months.

Folk magic has been used by the 'ordinary' population for centuries. It was my mother who introduced me to some of the elements of folk magic. This was gleaned by her from rural Surrey and the Isle of Man or (in a bit of a cliché) passed down through my grandmother. Mum would often tell us about simple charms to attract money, to see who you are to marry in the future, to see if a couple would stay together in their relationship, the odd charm to cure warts, and how a rowan tree in the garden will protect the house and so forth. Many people who are now of middle-aged years will remember similar things, such as a rabbit foot carried for luck (these were very popular in my school in the 1960s). A ladybird landing on you meant luck but it must not be brushed away, instead the old rhyme recited to encourage it to fly away, 'Ladybird, ladybird, fly away home, your house is on fire and your children are gone'. There is a wealth of other superstitions and charms concerning luck, many of which are still followed by schoolchildren and adults alike up until this day. Charms and superstitions of this sort were common to a fair sized portion of the population of the UK and Ireland and is what fuelled my interest in folk magic.

Accordingly the sort of magic that was often passed down by ordinary folk or through the cunning tradition and, although modernized, is still based on charms of old. I much prefer this simple way of working with magic to long complicated magical ritual gleaned from magi of the past that involves much in the way of study and skill. In the end, it is the power of thought, the belief and the intent of the charm, which causes it to work. Skill is still required but is more in the way of cooking a simple but nutritious meal than serving up a ten-course gourmet meal using the best crystal glasses, silver cutlery and Wedgewood dinner service.

In folk magic, the same as with any form of magic, the usual rules apply. This would include the law of return or something similar, or a personal ethic such as if you think what you are doing is wrong then it is. I do believe in some sort of comeback from spells cast.

In making a charm, I mainly use natural ingredients found in the lanes, fields and forest around me, but as a modern witch I have other items easily available to me, such as candles, essential oils, ribbons, material, string and kitchen herbs.

Most people want charms for love, luck, money and protection. Love charms to attract a certain person, I stay well away from, but I have made the odd charm to attract love in general, which is about the person themselves and not someone they may particularly want to attract.

The charms I make come in many forms; sachets, talismans, amulets and bunches of wildflowers and herbs. In my spells, which may be a little more involved, I will use a combination of ingredients perhaps such things as ribbons, herbs, candles, wildflowers, rune symbols, written words and chants. I do also incorporate moon phases.

Ritual

Although folk magic or simple spell work would not appear to warrant it, ritual does help put us in the mindset for magical purpose and it is a discipline that helps us reach into the invisible. A ritual works symbolically as each movement represents something. Symbols work on a conscious and subconscious level. In the case of the spell, the symbols work on both. However, ritual also reveals a mythic reality. What happens within the ritual is invisible (the altering of reality), a sort of sacred narrative working in the background, but of which the spell caster is conscious and believes in. Within the ritual, we pass through different stages of the spell in order to create it. All the time we are focused on the goal of the spell and have a heightened awareness of what is happening, this also helps in summoning up the invisible energies that make it work. However, as with all aspects of a folk charm this would also be in a simple form. Assembling my charm while concentrating on the goals I wish it to achieve are part of this, as is then taking it outside to my altar to further concentrate on the objective of the charm.

I do often call on nature spirits to aid in a charm. For instance if I have put together a charm in the way of a bunch of potent herbs for personal use or for a friend or a member of the family, I will then leave it on my outside altar which is a five foot high tree stump with lots of nooks and crannies in it. I might say a few words and concentrate on the aims of the charm, and then ask the nature spirits for their help, leaving them an offering. Alternatively, I will make up an offering of a few items and then ask the nature spirits for help in a certain matter.

Putting a Charm Together
When we cook, we know what foods complement each other and do not contradict in taste, otherwise the result would be awful. This comes with practice. Just as in a recipe, we can also construct a charm with ingredients that work the best together. Putting all the elements of a spell together, that is simple ritual, the ingredients, moon phases and the power of thought condense earthly and cosmic energies and are what

makes the spell complete.

In putting together a talisman, I might use a rune charm or some written words and infuse with this magical power to make it more potent. More often than not, I make a talisman out of herbs. This usual comes in the form of a bunch of herbs tied with string or particularly colored ribbon, or a sachet made with muslin.

Occasionally I will do something much simpler and pick up a naturally magical item to carry as an amulet. Again I will infuse this with magical powers for the person to wear or carry for instance as a passive protective charm. An example would be a sprig of rowan.

Many people cast a Circle for their own protection while spell working. Simpler 'folk magic' does not necessarily need a Circle. I personally do not use one for my simple charms. Circles are very much a personal choice.

I do tally my charms in with the moon phases, as I believe this has an influence on them, making them more powerful. A full moon is generally good for all kinds of magic, divining, and the raising of power, and is a good time to cast positive spells, such as success, protection, love, happiness, and health. The new moon is good for spells associated with new beginnings and money luck. The waxing moon occurs between the new moon and full moon, and is the best time to cast positive spells but particularly those of growth and change. The waning moon occurs between the full moon and new moon, and is the phase when it is best to cast negative spells such as ridding of bad habits, return of curses and binding spells.

Below is an example of a charm for protection if for instance someone is receiving much negative energy from another person.

Simple Protection Charm

Rowan
White Heather
Ivy
Holly

This bunch is collected from the wild in late summer and autumn. I collect the rowan when it is in berry and dry it for use all year round. I do the same with heather. As an evergreen, ivy is available throughout the year as is holly though if you want the berries you should wait until late autumn.

You or the person for whom the charm is intended should place it over the doorway of your or their home, or in a place you or they think needs protecting such as a place of work. Heather has a dual purpose in that it brings luck.

Tie the items into a bunch using black ribbon to repel negativity. You can do this at the place you will be leaving it, on your altar or Craft table, or out of doors during the full moon. Think about your goal, if it is for yourself then visualize the charm protecting you or your home or workplace with a pool of white light. If it is for someone else, then think of that person and infuse the bunch with white light, which will spread out when you give it to them. They will also need to believe in the charm to keep it potent.

You can chant words to help in the intent of the charm such as:

Full moon of the midnight
Infuse this charm with your light
Protect from harm and deflect negativity
Attract and encourage bright positivity

Keep the charm simple but the intent and will must be strong. You can read more about folk magic in the follow up book to this in the Pagan Portal series, *Hedge Magic.*

7

Divination

Intuition and Imagination

We are all intuitive although the strength of this may vary. Some of us will have naturally strong abilities, others less so but can learn to develop and keep inherent abilities keen.

Being aware of our intuitiveness has to be the responsibility of the individual as no one can do this for us. To bring back to full strength our inner senses buried deep within us having perhaps lost them as a child or teenager, will help us develop as a person and as a witch.

Learning to enhance your intuitiveness can help you be more aware of what goes on around you. It can help you 'see' and 'feel' more than you would normally. We have infinite possibilities to 'see' so much more than we do already, and this in turn can help us connect with spirit within and without.

Intuitiveness comes in a flash, is not planned, and we do not form it intentionally.

Ways of enhancing your intuition may include learning a divination skill, meditation and visualization, hedge riding, and practicing seeing auras. Become at one with nature, or living things within nature, such as trees. In doing this we tune in more to hidden feelings and thoughts, the trick then is to learn to trust and believe in them.

Imagination also has its place in the practices of the book. Imagination is limitless and has no restrictions except what we put there ourselves in a conscious act. Although when we 'imagine' we are building up a series of invented pictures in our minds, such as with visualization, this in turn can lead to more profound experiences. From the surface exercises of imagination, we can pass more deeply within ourselves and touch on our inner senses. This is often in the form of a trancelike state as we pass from full consciousness to a just below conscious state. What we imagine becomes real to us and it generally changes in form in a way that is no longer under our control — the narrative myth we have created becomes reality. We do not lose control of ourselves as we are conscious of what we do and we are aware that we can return to our normal environment, rather the scenery may change and we might meet people that we did not originally conjure up in our imaginations. This is part and parcel of hedge riding.

To enhance your intuitiveness, meditate or visualize regularly. Take up a form of divination such as tarot or runes (see my book *The Spiritual Runes*). Tasseomancy is a simple form of divination with only the cost of the loose tea. I remember talk of tealeaves being read in many an ordinary household during the 1950s and 60s, but the practice is much older than that. There are many more forms of divination, below are just two that suit the hedge witch very well.

Dowsing

You can make your own divining sticks or use a hazel twig, or make rods out of a coat hanger. To make a set you will need a wire coat hanger and wire cutters. Cut rods from two coat hangers and bend them into an L shape. I would suggest a length between twelve and sixteen inches for the longer part, and the shorter part between four and six inches. You then place the shorter lengths (the handles), into empty plastic pen cases so they can freely swing.

Hold the rods loosely in your fists. You should be relaxed and your arms and the arms of the rods held out horizontally and parallel to the ground. Your elbows should be kept close to your body. Move forward slowly and keep relaxed. You will find that shortly the rods will begin to move around, without you doing anything to cause it. When they find an energy center, they will cross over suddenly or open out into a V shape.

I use the rods in places where I see energy, mists, or feel any strange vibes as well as on ley lines or at sacred sites. Using the rods can help you develop your psychic awareness as you can test any strange vibes you may come across.

You can also dowse with a pendulum. You can buy a pendulum and there are many on offer, with some made of metal and some of crystal. You need to hold the end of the thread or chain with your index finger and thumb, holding it very steady so as not to influence the way it swings. Rest your elbow on a table to help keep it steady.

Generally, you ask a question of the pendulum. Before using it you need to establish which way it swings for 'yes' and which way for 'no'.

Scrying

Try scrying using a crystal ball, black mirror or water, though you can also scry into fire.

To make a black mirror, use a photo frame, (one with a black casing is best) and you will need a can of black spray paint. Remove the glass from the frame and spray the back of it. Once dry replace the glass in the frame and you are ready to go.

For water scrying, use a black bowl and fill it with water or stare into a dark pool of water or lake taking care not to fall in. You can even scry in a puddle.

If you are indoors, keep the room fairly dark and it also needs to be quiet. Any candles should be out of your line of vision. Make sure you are sitting comfortably as you will be in the same position for some time. Sit and gaze into the crystal ball, mirror or bowl. It helps if your eyes go slightly out of focus such as when you look at a magic eye picture. After a while, you will become trancelike. This can bring forth images, which may be in the form of symbols. With this, thoughts may pop into your mind, connected with what you see. It is what they mean to you that counts, so when interpreting them later, try to avoid looking up their meanings in a book.

You may receive several images accompanied by thoughts, and they may build up into a narrative, which gives you a message, or explains something that has been puzzling you, providing a solution to a problem or helping you make a decision.

At first, it can be frustrating if you do not 'see' anything. Be patient and keep trying and you will eventually achieve success.

8

Journal: The Seasons

Autumn

Cave

This morning I rose bright and early as I was going with two friends to the hermitage, cave and well. The wind was howling and the rain battering the windows. When it was time to leave all was quiet again. It started to rain just as we arrived. It was a twenty-minute walk to the cave. We changed into our walking boots, wrapped up for the weather, and set off. It was not too bad as we scrambled up the slippery slope past the hermitage ruins and up to the cave. We lit a few nightlights and made ourselves comfortable with the cushions and blankets we had brought with us. The rain began in earnest and the wind rushed through the hazel wood outside the cave.

I started the pathworking by leading the others through the cave and out into the wood, and then we carried it on ourselves.

Later we each told of our experiences then blew out our nightlights and collecting them up we walked down to the well. I bathed my hands in the cool clear stream and we each drank some of the water. By now, it was raining hard and by the time we reached the car, we were all soaked through but exhilarated. We went back to the house for a warm drink and to dry off.

Irish Moss

The day was sunny but cool and I went with my husband to

the beach to look for Irish moss otherwise known as *chondrus crispus*, for some spell work. Irish moss is a type of seaweed found around the coast. On the way, we were stuck with some other traffic behind a donkey and cart on a bridge and managed to have a good look at the waterfalls there. The water was high and gushing furiously down the falls, as we had recently had heavy rain.

At the beach, I had put on my wellington boots and paddled through a few inches of water to reach the rocks. I soon spotted some of the seaweed and began to collect it. After a while, the sea seemed to be sweeping in and the channel of water I had waded through was now too deep for me. I hurried over the rocks slipping and sliding, which is no mean feat for someone with an inner ear problem and terrible balance. I at last found a shallow pool and waded through it jumping onto the sand with a wail of triumph only to find my husband had filmed the whole thing.

We had a lovely walk along the beach, and I collected some shells and a few pebbles for my Irish set of runes I was intending to make. After picking up some litter as usual we came back home. We stopped off at the falls and took a riverside walk, and it was so wonderful listening to the thundering water. I acknowledged the faeries of the water and we returned home. Excited with my first harvest of Irish moss, I was at first disappointed then highly amused when I discovered I had collected false Irish moss. Well, at least it would lead to another expedition, so I set about looking for uses for false Irish moss instead.

Winter

Walks

Cold frosty morning followed by winter sunshine is my favorite type of winter day. I cannot wait to go out for a daily walk in perhaps the woods or lanes. At this time of year, November to December, the woodland paths are thick with bronze, golden and yellow leaves, and it is a pleasurable experience walking through them.

Robins seem to be plentiful now and, if I am lucky, I will spot a red squirrel in the trees, or hear the wildlife in the undergrowth. If I stay until dark, I may spot a deer among the trees.

This is a good time to collect kindling for the fire, as often we have windy days. To come home to a blazing fire, with a warm cup of cocoa, mulled wine or hot toddy is bliss.

Today is one of those days, so I am off out.

Spring

Litter Rant
Down our remote country lane among the beautiful pine is the perfect place for you to dump your litter. Old chest freezers, furniture that is past its sell by date, even bags of household waste can be dumped. And you walkers who love to dress up in your walking boots and waterproofs and tramp up the lane and on the designated forest walks bragging about your healthy ways, why not throw your empty drink cans and plastic bottles into the hedgerows and verges. I love to take a bag down and collect them to put into my recycling, which I have to pay for. So feel free to come our way and dump away ... NOT!

Signs of Activity
I have been wildlife spotting and so far have seen a brown hare and a pheasant running through the garden. Nearby there was a red squirrel running up a pine tree.

I love the yellow of spring in April heralding good things to come. On one walk up the lane, I saw daffodils, primroses, celandine, dandelions, furze and forsythia.

Spotting new wildflowers is a pastime of mine. In each area where I have lived, there are different species as the terrain varies. I take a good look at them, take a photo if I have a camera and identify them when I get back to the house. Today I saw wood sorrel and a purple flower I have yet to identify. I need to take a closer look at the leaf.

Summer

Bealtaine

We were invited down to Castle Pook in County Cork, which is only an hour away, to join in a small private celebration.

We socialized first, eating a lovely meal outdoors. After eating, we moved on to the guesthouse to warm ourselves. When it grew dark, we walked down the field to the fire. It was a cool evening and the fire was warming. The night was clear and the sky filled with stars as it was not polluted with light. We held hands and the ritual was simple but lovely, the way I like it, with meaningful words said. Some jumped the balefire and we stayed for a while to stargaze.

After returning to the guesthouse for more celebrations, we watched out for the moon rising. She was soon spotted and once more we went outside to watch Lady Moon as touched by the sun she came up a great orange ball over the horizon. The rest of the evening was spent in celebration and in the morning we breakfasted together.

A lovely Bealtaine, time spent with hospitable and wise friends.

Summer Solstice

The summer solstice was a quiet affair this year with two family weddings in one month, so I celebrated by placing a candle lantern in the old tree stump, along with a few gifts for the wee folk, and paid homage to the Earth Mother.

Now in July, it is so lovely to see the lanes filled with foxglove, wild fuchsia, meadowsweet and fragrant honeysuckle. The flowers are out on the elder so this week I shall make some elderflower cordial. There are plenty of flowers on the bramble too, so there should be a good harvest of blackberries this year. The sloe berries are beginning to form so I have made a mental note not just to make sloe gin but also to make fuchsia and blackberry jam come autumn. The rose bushes by the gate have now produced a mass of peachy colored roses. Along with the *rosa rugosa* already in the garden, and some dog roses in the lanes, I should be able to collect enough hips to make some rosehip tea for some time to come. It is going to be a busy autumn.

My lettuce, rocket and peashoots have provided a few lovely salads but the poor parsley was attacked by white fly, so now I need to look into companion planting.

I love being a hedge witch, it is what I am all about.

Moon Books invites you to begin or deepen your encounter with Paganism, in all its rich, creative, flourishing forms.